SOUTHERN GRIT

SOUTHERN GRIT

Sensing the Siege at Petersburg

Michael Martin

SHOTWELL PUBLISHING
Columbia, So. Carolina

SOUTHERN GRIT: SENSING THE SIEGE AT PETERSBURG
Copyright © 2018 by Michael Martin

ALL RIGHTS RESERVED. No part of this publication may be reproduced, distributed, or transmitted in any form or by any means, including photocopying, recording, or other electronic or mechanical methods, or by any information storage and retrieval system without the prior written permission of the publisher, except in the case of very brief quotations embodied in critical reviews and certain other non-commercial uses permitted by copyright law.

Produced in the REPUBLIC OF SOUTH CAROLINA by

SHOTWELL PUBLISHING, LLC
Post Office Box 2592
Columbia, South Carolina 29202

www.ShotwellPublishing.com

Cover: "Soldier Fellow # 1" by James W. Johnson | jameswjohnson.com
Cover Design: Hazel's Dream / Boo Jackson TCB

ISBN-13: 978-1947660045
ISBN-10: 1947660047

10 9 8 7 6 5 4 3 2 1

Contents

Introduction: Federal Terror in Our Everyday Thoughts vii

Notes on the Sources xv

Chapter One: Younger Longest and the 26th Virginia 1

Chapter 2: The Perception of Slavery Among Virginians 6

Chapter 3: The Blending of Education and Confederate Nationalism 11

Chapter 4: How Did Virginia Perceive the Confederate Flag? 16

Chapter 5: Sight, Sounds, and Civilians at the Siege of Petersburg 26

Chapter 6: Younger Longest at the Crater 31

Chapter 7: The Sight and Smell of Terror 40

Chapter 8: Virginia Tasting Defeat 46

Chapter 9: Southerners in a Cold World 53

About the Author 63

INTRODUCTION
Federal Terror in Our Everyday Thoughts

AROUND THE TIME I DISCOVERED my Confederate ancestors, I started to become fascinated with metacognition, which is most simply defined as "thinking about thinking." In school I always loved American history, particularly the War Between the States (WBTS), but was never taught to examine it beneath the textbook, reconstructed narrative of the "Civil War." Most of my teachers and professors taught the typical story of how the war was primarily over slavery. There was never any real discussion or focus on the South as a region or its people. To be sure, I was made to think the South was something of a cultural wasteland. That all changed when I discovered my heritage and began reading things that Southerners actually wrote.

Years of study taught me that Southerners were keen, intuitive people with an appreciation for the mind and its higher faculties. Research began for this book by studying my own family history, but soon expanded to the towns they lived in, the regiments they fought in, and the things their neighbors wrote about. Eventually, I realized that the South was a lot more distinctive and intellectual than I had been led to believe. I had to know more. I became determined to learn what my ancestor and his comrades were fighting for in the 1860s. Every sensory perception I was reading about took on a new, profound importance. Most of all, in the wake of all the drama over Confederate flags and monuments being removed, I started to wonder if maybe the Southern side of things had been left out for a reason. Maybe the government does not want us to know what Confederates were fighting for....

After doing a lot research, I learned some fascinating information about the mind and about the Southern people in general.

Did you know that experts are now beginning to understand just how fast our thoughts travel? Studies have shown that thoughts travel around 830,000 miles an hour; to put that in perspective, thoughts travel about 936,000 times faster than the sound of our voice. Our thoughts are real, so powerful that they could travel from pole to pole, around the earth in less than a second. People recognize this power from time to time, but rarely try to harness their thoughts. For example, have you ever walked into a room, looked at someone, and "felt" some kind of connection? Have you ever "felt" fear or love? Those "feelings" are the vibrations that your thoughts are sending through the body.[1] I believe that our ancestors'—white, black, northern, southern—thoughts and feelings were so powerful, that we may be experiencing them all the time. In particular, I believe that our "Civil War" ancestors had thoughts and experiences that are still reverberating *all around us.*

The goal of *Southern Grit* is to analyze the senses, thoughts, and actions of Confederates during the Siege of Petersburg and let the

---

[1] Bob Proctor, "The 11 Forgotten Laws," Lecture, https://www.youtube.com/watch?v=1MbuyN3vfx0, May 15, 2016.

reader determine what was driving the minds of typical Southern soldiers. *Southern Grit* is dedicated to my 4th great grandfather, Younger Longest, as well as all the other Southerners who fought by his side at Petersburg. Discovering Younger's letters, from a time when many men were illiterate, confirmed my life's work as a historian and writer. I truly believe that somehow he planted the seeds that would make me interested in history. I also think that somehow he may have been guiding me this whole time to find the story he left behind.

After learning my family history, several problems and philosophical quibbles arose in my mind. I began to question the entire world around me when I started to think of it from my ancestor's perspective. All of the hottest media topics, and even the foundation of my knowledge, began to seem abstract when I thought of them through my ancestor's lens. I realized that all my ideas about the Confederate flag, terrorism, and other modern "political" issues were completely based on what I had been told, not based on things that actually happened in the past. My ancestors showed me — and I will strive to prove to all readers in this book — that the American people had a lot of grit compared to the average person today. During the Siege of Petersburg, Southern soldiers and civilians alike endured horrendous conditions in defense of their homeland. It was a battle for their very minds. The bravery and fortitude with which they faced a larger and better equipped opponent deserves closer attention.

Today, in 2017, we live in a day and age where Americans are basically defenseless against terror. People face violence at almost any public place they go. When did terrorism against civilians become so pervasive in our culture? Mass shootings, police brutality, and bombings have become routine in our society. Most people think this slaughter of innocent people is a relatively recent phenomenon in America. I became fascinated to learn that my ancestors had a weapon of mass destruction, planted by the United States in an act of terror, detonated under them while they were sleeping in 1864 during the Siege of Petersburg. This made me question everything I THOUGHT I knew about terror and the "Civil War."

Ultimately, "terrorism" is a word that has constantly been remolded to provide Americans with an *enemy image*. Some political theorists, like Carl Schmitt, have held the theory that a society cannot be complete without this enemy image. Throughout American history, our society has come together when we have a common enemy—some recent examples might be the surge of patriotism after the Pearl Harbor bombing and the 9/11 terrorist attacks. Even going all the way back to our founding fathers, we can clearly see that Americans were united in their contempt for British policies. Our cause was so uplifted, and our hatred for the enemy image of Britain was so strong, we are willing to overlook the fact that the founding fathers basically engaged in terrorism. If a group like the Sons of Liberty existed today, meeting in secret, using violence and intimidation, and tarring and feathering people, they would be considered terrorists.

Because the South is the only region of America that has lost a war, and because it has historically been portrayed as the *enemy image* of the WBTS, Americans have overlooked the fact that the South was undeniably the victim of Northern terrorism. The Siege of Petersburg is the perfect place to explore this idea. A once bustling hub for the railroad industry, Petersburg was the last stronghold between the Union army and the Confederate capital of Richmond and the place that protected the railroads that supplied the Confederate army. The city was slowly destroyed through questionable tactics. Since it was completely acceptable for the United States to starve and bomb Petersburg's innocent people, Federals dug in and took to siege tactics. They did so mainly because it was election year in 1864.

The leader of the Union army, Ulysses S. Grant, had experience crushing Southern cities. At Vicksburg he shelled innocents and starved the city, strangling it like a living being. With Lincoln running for re-election, Grant was not seeking peace nor fighting any more of the very costly blundering battles that he had been fighting. Instead, he chose to dig in and strangle another Southern city. Grant's army also implemented new, unexpected tactics like undermining and blowing up Confederate soldiers in their sleep. At the same time, to truly break the hearts and minds of Southerners, Federals like William T. Sherman were engaged in "total war" by destroying Southern civilians' means of living.

If Abraham Lincoln's entire plan was to "preserve the Union," how could he have approved such things? His first war action was a proclamation on April 15, 1861, calling for 75,000 militia to serve 90 days to "suppress ... combinations too powerful to be suppressed by the ordinary course of judicial proceedings." Lincoln never referred to Confederate States or Confederates—always to rebels. This means, in his mind, he was quashing a rebellion of certain lawless citizens, not fighting a war between nations. If he viewed the Confederates as rebels, not a sovereign nation, then that means he was deliberately fighting to coerce a huge segment of the American people. If Lincoln was willing to blow up "rebels" and civilians indiscriminately over their interpretation of the Constitution, then was he not a terrorist by today's definition? I think it is time to re-think what we know about terrorism. If one were to look at how America currently defines terrorism and then took the time to examine our own past, a lot of questions start to arise.

Our current, U.S. Code of Federal Regulations' definition of terrorism reads:

> The unlawful use of force and violence against persons or property to intimidate or coerce a government, the civilian population, or any segment thereof, in furtherance of political or social objectives.[2]

By that modern definition, the United States was certainly using terrorist tactics against the South during the WBTS. The entire effort of the United States was focused on coercing the Southern states into subjugation. Furthermore, the Federal government brought the war to civilians in extreme ways, for political and social objectives. Even less violent Union tactics like the blockade were widely recognized by international law as instruments of war between *sovereign* nations.

After exploring the senses of Confederates at Petersburg, I make the argument that Southerners were undoubtedly the victims of

---

[2] Code of Federal Regulations 28, Sec. 85.

terrorism. From a purely sensory perspective, Confederates faced threats very similar to what modern people face in our current "War on Terror."

Notes on the Sources

THIS BOOK IS A SENSORY HISTORY, not a comprehensive work on the WBTS or the Siege of Petersburg. It must be understood that what happened at Petersburg was a nine-month battle of attrition. Petersburg was a major rail center and one of the last major defenses before the Confederate capital of Richmond.

The focus here will be specifically what was in the *mind* of Southerners at Petersburg and what they sensed. In all, Confederates withstood nine Union offensives and two cavalry raids, repelling the larger Union forces several times. The most famous engagement, which we will examine closely, was the Battle of the Crater on July 30, 1864. In one of the most devious attacks ever, Union soldiers dug a tunnel and detonated a mine underneath Confederate forces. Afterward, the chaos which ensued was referred to by U.S. Grant as "the saddest affair I have witnessed in the war."

Several books have been written both about the Siege of Petersburg and the Battle of the Crater, detailing troop movements and engagements. Books like *In the Trenches at Petersburg* and *The Last Citadel* extensively cover what happened at Petersburg as far as concerns fortifications and engagements, but lack comprehensive details on Southerners and what they were experiencing. *Southern Grit* hopes to breathe humanity into the Southerners at Petersburg and examine what happened from their sensory perspectives.

Michael Martin

Many people have wondered what it would be like to fight in a battle of this magnitude. We will focus on Southerners, like Younger Longest, who were there and examine their *sensory* experiences—what they saw, smelled, tasted, and felt. Careful attention will also be placed on their religious thoughts and ideas.

What motivated Confederates to fight with such tenacity? What were the real ideals they were fighting for in the face of danger? Looking inside the mind of Younger Longest and his comrades will give us a better understanding of how Confederates operated on conscious and sub-conscious levels. We live in a society today dominated by a powerful federal government. As a nation, we may never again see our own people take arms over governmental principles. Whether or not you think this is a good or bad thing, it is something Confederates were willing to do. For that reason and for many others, their thoughts and actions deserve examination.

CHAPTER ONE

Younger Longest & the 26th Virginia

TO BETTER UNDERSTAND the mindset of Younger Longest, his long journey through the Civil War should be examined in detail. Below is a table displaying his Virginia Regiment's history.[3]

Late June 1861	The King and Queen County Guards arrived at Gloucester Point on the Steamer Logan. They and other Companies from the counties of Gloucester and Mathews formed the 26th Regiment Virginia Volunteers
July 1, 1861	The Regiment was mustered into Confederate service with ten companies. First mission was to support naval battery at Gloucester Point and defend Gloucester County.
Dec. 18, 1861	Younger Longest enrolled by Col. P. R. Page at Gloucester Point.
May 4, 1862	The Regiment left Gloucester Point to defend Richmond and was sent to Chaffin's Bluff on the Henrico County side of the James River.
June 30, 1862	Moved to near New Market and was briefly involved in the skirmish there.
July 2, 1862	Moved back to Chaffin's Bluff on Burton's farm where they drilled and gardened.

---

[3] H. Earl Longest and Gladys B. Longest, *The History of the Longest Family, 1652 – 1992*. St. Stephens Church, 1992.

MICHAEL MARTIN

April 8, 1863	Moved down the Peninsula to Williamsburg and briefly engaged Federals.
April 23, 1863	Back at Burton's Farm.
August 5, 1863	Moved to Deep Bottom on the James River to attack Federal Gunboats. Boats escaped.
Sept. 19, 1863	Arrived at Charleston by rail and was stationed at Wappoo four miles west of Charleston.
Feb. 10, 1864	Engaged Federals near Charleston. Federals retreated.
Late Feb., 1864	Regiment ordered to Lake City, FL, by rail. Was detoured a few days at Savannah, GA, to back up defense there, then on to FL.
April 17, 1864	Ordered back to Charleston by rail Stationed at James Island in defense of Charleston.
May 3, 1864	Regiment ordered to Richmond.
May 7, 1864	Part of Regiment ordered to Nottoway Bridge and engaged Federals who burned bridge. One member of the 26th killed in this action.
May 10, 1864	Regiment arrived at Petersburg
May 19, 1864	26th involved with pushing Gen. Benjamin F. Butler's Union Force back to Bermuda Neck. The 26th lost 2 killed and 48 wounded.
June 9, 1864	Regiment returned to Petersburg.
June 15, 1864	Parts of 3 companies in the 26th captured by 13th New Hampshire Regiment in a battle for Confederate Battery 5 defending Petersburg.
July 10, 1864	Younger's brother Howard killed in action by mortar fire in Petersburg.
July 30, 1864	Battle of the Crater saw 26th VA Regiment holding back Federal divisions in the breach of the Confederate line caused by the crater. The Regiment suffered heavy losses. Siege in trenches continued.
Dec. 8, 1864	Younger's cousin, Private John Longest, killed in the trenches by a minie ball during the continued siege of Petersburg.
March 31, 1865	Younger was captured at Hatcher's Run.

April 2, 1865	Younger was listed as a POW at Point Lookout, Maryland.
April 12, 1865	Robert E. Lee surrendered the army of Northern Virginia.
June 29, 1865	Younger was released and took the Oath of Allegiance.

For a better understanding of the force Longest traveled with, examine the following description of the regiment, consisting initially of 10 companies of 150 men each:

Company A- the York River Rifles- Captain Joshua L. Garrett

Company B- the Gloucester Grays- Captain Patrick Fitzhugh

Company C- the King and Queen Minute Men- Captain Napoleon B. Street

Company D- the Mathews Men- Captain Alexander James

Company E- the Lincoln Hunters- Captain John Perrin

Company F- the Gloucester Invincibles- Captain William Perrin

Company G- the Clifton Guards- Captain R. H. Spencer

Company H- the King and Queen Guards- Captain Robert Sutton

Company I- the Jackson Grays- Captain James C. Councill (Younger's Regiment)[4]

Company J- from Halifax County- Captain A. W. Poindexter

The 26th Virginia was a volunteer regiment, which means that Younger Longest and the rest of the soldiers were at first armed with their own weapons, mainly flintlock muskets. Their first mission was to defend the Naval battery at Gloucester Point, and the first months were spent drilling and building fortifications. Around 450 local slaves raised from the county did much of the labor. The regiment saw no real military action in the first year of the war. Soldiers were living well and frequently received family visits, but most men were ready for action.

Unfortunately, the regiment suffered heavily from mumps, measles, typhoid, and malaria due to overcrowding and poor sanitary conditions.

It was not until the regiment was ordered to defend Petersburg in May 1864 that it saw major action. In one battle during the Siege of Petersburg, June 15-18, 1864, the 26th lost companies A, B, and G in the early stages. Younger and the rest of the regiment remained

---

[4] We will later explain why the Company was called the "Jackson Greys."

in the trenches until the Northern breakthrough in March 1865. On April 2, Gen. Robert E. Lee's army left the Petersburg trenches headed west. These men had been in the trenches just a few days short of ten months — surely a test of endurance.

On April 8, 1865, the 26th Regiment reached the Appomattox Court House, just one day before Lee's surrender. Just days earlier, Younger Longest had been captured at a small battle near Petersburg called Hatcher's Run. While Younger was a POW at Point Lookout, his regiment surrendered their flag and their arms, returned to camp and were paroled. Each man had to take the Oath of Allegiance to the U.S. Government, "to protect and defend it" and never to bear arms against it.

The roster of the 26th shows 62 men killed in action, 23 mortally wounded, and 138 dead by disease (dysentery and diarrhea were the biggest killers). Sixty-seven men were discharged with some type of physical disability. With the lack of adequate medical supplies, food, clothing, and ammunition, it is surprising there were not more casualties. Younger Longest survived the war.

Chapter 2
The Perception of Slavery Among Virginians

NOW THAT WE HAVE a basic understanding of the events Younger Longest went through, we shall turn our attention to events that may have shaped him in the years leading to the Civil War. With extensive research on Younger Longest's background, a variety of sources provide information about his life before the war. Digging through Virginia archives and historical society collections provides information that in 1848 he worked as an overseer for a local planter named John Walker. Walker farmed about 400 acres and often hired neighborhood men to live with him and assist with business.

Overseers were a middle ground between planters and slaves. They often lived modestly in small houses and were paid partly in farm produce to supplement their own production, or sometimes they were paid in credit at nearby stores. Their days often consisted of assembling workers at dawn, supervising their meals, overseeing the care of the stock, visiting and treating the sick, and inspecting quarters for cleanliness (on Sundays).

Walker tried to hire honest sons of poor farmers as overseers; however, low wages combined with low social standing made filling the job difficult. This meant that flexibility was very important; in fact, Walker always said that the overseer could quit or be dismissed at any time. Younger Longest worked on Walker's farm for less than two weeks when he left "on his own accord thinking, he said, he could not manage negroes."[5]

Walker recorded the following regarding overseers:

> If he thinks or knows he can't attend to my business and thinks he ought, he is at liberty to quit me ... If on the other hand I should find him incompetent to attend my business as an overseer, I am at liberty to discharge him.[6]

Overseers on Walker's farm worked only temporarily after Younger Longest, as indicated by the turnover rate. No details are given as to the exact problems Longest encountered. He was paid $1.50 for his time. Perhaps Younger did not have the stomach to be an overseer. As a group, overseers were generally reputed to be unreliable and dishonest.

---

[5] Bulletin of the King and Queen County Historical Society of Virginia, No. 78 (1962)

[6] *Ibid*. Overseers were hired seasonally. Salaries were negotiated for each season. Overseers also frequently received a place to live, food, and other advantages.

Overseers of John Walker at Chatham Hill		
Date	Overseer	Salary
1825	William Cook	$53.30
1840	Robert Edwards	$80.00
1847	Richard Lumpkin	$60.00
1848	Younger Longest	$60.00
1849		
1850	W.J. and Edwin Watkins	$50.00
1851	Lewis Ball	$40.00
Mar 1851	W.J. Watkins	$45.00
Jan 1852	Franklin Simpkins	$50.00
Aug 1852	John F. Simpkins	$60.00
Aug 1853	Philip Trice	$60.00
1854	Philip Trice	$60.00

Was Younger one of the bad overseers? Or did he, as the son of a small farmer, hope that being an overseer would lead towards a plantation of his own someday? The latter is very likely; in the 1850 census, most of the 18,859 overseers in the South were on large plantations. Only about 11% worked on smaller farms the size of Walker's. Unless someone is willing to devote a lifetime of research, we may never know the exact type of man Younger Longest was before the war. However, it is clear that Younger started as an overseer and that, for some reason, he did not want to manage slaves.

The fact is that slavery was sometimes a dangerous field to be involved in. During September of 1663, Gloucester County (where Younger Longest enlisted) was home to one of the first American slave rebellions. White indentured servants and black slaves plotted a major conspiracy but were betrayed to authorities. Several conspirators were beheaded. Nat Turner's revolt in 1831, also in Virginia, resulted in the murder of approximately 60 whites, mostly children, and the eventual execution of many blacks.

Some saw slavery as a "divine institution," some saw it as economic opportunity, many saw it as evil—but all Americans profited from it in different ways. Historians rarely note the danger that was present for all parties involved. A great example would be seen in the records of the Fleet family, neighbors of Younger Longest, whose sons fought in Younger's regiment. A letter from Dr. Benjamin Fleet to his son Fred in 1863 shows how dangerous the "divine institution" still was, almost 200 years after the first slave rebellion in America:

> Feb 3, 1863 ... A most brutal murder was committed by one of Wm: or P. H. Aylett's negroes on Friday night of the overseer, who, by the way, is the same man that Frank Dew had at Malvern Hill last year, his name is Pitts, & I understand he has always borne an excellent character. He gave him a slight correction and the negro went into one of the quarters mouthing him and making many threats of vengeance against him. When Pitts attempted to go into the house, just as he entered the door, the boy fell aboard of him with a large wagon pin, knocking him senseless to the floor, & repeating his blows after Pitts was prostrate, until he supposed he had finished him. Poor Pitts, I hear,

survived until yesterday when he died, at least such is the news Mr. Wilson brings from Dunkirk this morning . . . .[7]

Many people like to imagine slavery as a highly regarded institution where whites savagely beat slaves, something the letter by Dr. Fleet contradicts. The truth, somewhere in between, is that violence impacted the perceptions of innocent people on all sides and prevented any type of real compromise on ending slavery.

---

[7] Betsy Fleet and John D.P. Fuller, eds., *Green Mount: A Virginia Plantation Family During the Civil War* (Charlottesville: University Press of Virginia, 1962), p. 220.

Chapter 3
The Blending of Education and Confederate Nationalism

MANY FAMOUS PEOPLE, from all walks of life, find inspiration in teachers. James Calvin Councill was a teacher in King and Queen County. He was educated at Virginia Military Institute, which provided him the very best preparation for being an instructor. He taught for several years at an academy named Fleetwood and later at his own academy known as Aberdeen. During his time, Councill inspired many young people, sometimes working with up to forty students, aged anywhere from 10 to 20. Some boarded at the school and many were restless. Fred Fleet, a student of Councill's and later a soldier in his regiment, had the following to say about Councill's teaching methods:

> I think I can safely say that … I have never seen a school in which better order was preserved or where the boys as a whole were kept more steadily engaged at their work. And yet he conducted things so quietly and so simply that

no one seemed to realize that a master hand was at the helm.[8]

Fred Fleet, who served in the same regiment as Younger Longest, also described Councill as having "complete mastery" of his math subject. Councill never sat while teaching: he always stood, walking up and down the classroom with "his eyes on the floor, listening closely to the demonstration of a problem in arithmetic or algebra, or a proposition in geometry, without a book in his hand – or - what seemed at that time an incomprehensible mystery – without even taking up the book to see if the pupil had worked the problem correctly and had got the right answer!"[9] Imagine a teacher in our time who would not rely on textbooks. Standards and classroom size make that type of engagement difficult today, which is probably a reason that Councill was so influential to his students .

Councill was also a firm disciplinarian, and the students respected him for it. According to Fleet, "no one dared to disobey him, but they had the profoundest respect for him and unbounded admiration for his skill as a teacher." The teaching style of Councill

---

[8] Bulletin of the King and Queen County Historical Society, No. 16 (1964). Article written in 1905 when Councill's former pupils raised the money to erect a monument for his grave.

[9] *Ibid.*

was completely contradictory to what teachers do today; not only would he deviate from textbooks, but he would also punish students if they were not accountable. In a letter to his parents, Fred Fleet detailed how strict Councill's expectations were:

> Wednesday evening July 18th 1860 ... There was an eclipse of the Sun this morning, from 7 ½ until 9 o'clock, it was a very great one. Mr. Councill slapped one of the boys (Clark) three times in the hand, he is only one boy he has whipped since his school commenced. He told him last Friday, if he did not know some 5 or 6 tables in Arithmetic, he would whip him, but he played truant Monday & Tuesday & came today and did not know them & Mr. Councill slapped him with a Ruler.[10]

Councill's influence was just as strong after the South had begun to secede. On April 19, 1861, the first regiment to respond to Lincoln's call for troops (the 6th Massachusetts) tried to pass through Baltimore on its way to Washington. These Northern troops were met by a mob of ten thousand people. Shots were fired. Twelve citizens were killed and many wounded and four soldiers killed. Three days later Fred Fleet wrote the following:

---

[10] *Green Mount*, p. 27.

> Monday evening April 22, 1861. Councill went to the Court House today; they ordered out the Cavalry … and the militia including Pa will have to go the Court House, and I do not know where from thence. The school I reckon will be broken up this week if not sooner.[11]

Councill's time at Virginia Military Institute, combined with his years as a devoted teacher, made him an natural leader for the Confederate army. "When I had finished all my examinations and come back home around the 15th of June, 1861," wrote Fleet, "I found a company of my neighbors and friends had been raised for service in the Confederate Army, and that naturally all eyes turned to Mr. Council as its captain."[12] The belief in Councill was an appropriate leader for the local men was strong. The mothers, sisters, and friends of soldiers gathered at the nearby church to make coarse gray uniforms for the new company.

Council helped establish a company of volunteers out of the area where Fred Fleet and Younger Longest lived; it was mustered into the CSA as Company I, Twenty-Sixth Regiment of Virginia Volunteers. Later, Councill would rise to be Lieutenant Colonel of

---

[11] *Ibid.*, p. 29.

[12] Bulletin of the King and Queen County Historical Society, No. 17 (1964).

the 26th Virginia. As a teacher he was unparalleled, even by today's standards, in terms of engaging methods and content mastery. When the Confederacy was forming and the Union began invading the South, many young men looked to Councill for leadership. Although Younger Longest does not directly mention Councill, the fact that Younger served in his regiment and the fact that Councill was so prominent in local writings suggest that he may have been an influential force in Younger's life.

CHAPTER 4
How Did Virginia Perceive the Confederate Flag?

WHEN THINKING OF MARTYRS, particularly in regard to the Civil War, many people tend to think of John Brown. Authors like Ralph Waldo Emerson and Robert Penn Warren portray Brown as everything from Jesus to the Antichrist. Very few historians or writers focus on James W. Jackson, a true martyr, universally viewed as a hero in the South, for his refusal to let a Confederate flag be removed from atop his business. The true definition of martyr is someone who is killed for his or her beliefs. Delving into this definition further, we will examine why James Jackson was more of an actual martyr than John Brown. We will also consider how Jackson's martyrdom impacted Younger Longest and other Southerners. Finally, we will examine why Jackson's death is still relevant today.

James W. Jackson was the youngest of seven children born to Richard and Jane Jackson. James was tall and stout with prominent features and a handsome face. Most of the town folk of Alexandria considered him to be the strongest man and the best fighter of the community. Jackson was also very much a secessionist and loved the South. When the election of 1860 was taking place, he was "ever bold to denounce and prompt to punish any word of apology for

Abraham Lincoln and his insane party, however great the threatened detriment to his own interests in consequence."[13]

Jackson had made a name for himself by being hyper-vigilant in the months leading to the Civil War. He rushed to Harper's Ferry during John Brown's raid, hoping for action, but did not arrive in time. When Federals raised a Lincoln flag pole in Occoquan, Virginia, Jackson took part in cutting it down and kept the flag as a trophy. Legend says that he carried one of John Brown's pikes with a piece of John Brown Jr.'s ear on it. To put it simply, Jackson had become a model for "true sons of the South." He inspired those around him to protect the South from threatening outsiders.

On May 23, 1861, Virginia officially seceded from the Union and joined the Confederacy. The next day, Federal troops under Col. Elmer Ellsworth moved to occupy the city of Alexandria, Virginia. In his last letter to his parents, Ellsworth wrote:

Camp Lincoln. Washington DC, May 23, 1861

---

[13] Andrew D. White, *Life of James W. Jackson, the Alexandria Hero, the Slayer of Ellsworth, the First Martyr in the Cause for Southern Independence* (Richmond: West & Johnson, 1862), p. 13. This is practically the only source for Jackson's life and for the flag incident.

We have no means of knowing what type of reception we are to meet with. I am of the opinion that our entrance to the city of Alexandria will be hotly contested ... it may be my lot to be injured in some manner. Whatever may happen, cherish the consolation that I was engaged in a sacred duty.[14]

Ellsworth had a good reason to anticipate injury. He had seen a large Confederate flag flying over the city for some time. To Federals, this flag represented the growing boldness of the Confederacy. For James W. Jackson, the owner of the flag, it was an expression of his own convictions. He loved the South so much that he placed a forty-foot pole on top of his business, a hotel called The Marshall House, and flew the Confederate flag "as a proclamation of a faith, the emblem of a nationality, and the tutelary protection of cherished rights." The flag had long been a subject in the Northern press, and people joked often about how soon "Master Abe" would come and tear down his flag. Whenever someone referred to cutting the flag down, Jackson would almost always reply, "Then there

---

[14] http:/hdl.handle.net/10822/550604. Ellsworth led the 11th New York Regiment, known as "Fire Zouaves" because they came from the New York City fire department and wore gaudy uniforms copied after French colonial troops.

would be two dead men about when that flag came down."[15] Little did Jackson know that Elmer Ellsworth, a Federal Colonel and personal friend of Abe Lincoln, would soon put him to the test.

Despite the tense and uncertain atmosphere, Ellsworth marched into Alexandria after Virginia's secession, expecting trouble but finding his movement uncontested. Ellsworth's Zouave soldiers were described as extremely unwelcome:

> Their fantastic dress, the gleam of their sword bayonets, the investment of <u>terror</u> with which the braggadocio of the North had clothed them, all conspired to make them as they came up on the double quick, an omen of direful passage.[16]

After marching throughout the city to occupy the railroad and telegraph offices, the Zouave soldiers began removing anything "offensive" with the words "Southern." First, they found a sign that said "Southern Protection Insurance Company," removed it and threw it from a second story window. Next, they found a sign for a publication called "Southern Churchman," and proceeded to remove and demolish it. As if this gratuitous destruction was not

---

[15] White, p. 32.

[16] *Ibid.*

enough, Ellsworth then decided to take some men to the top of The Marshall House and cut down the large Confederate flag. Jackson had been asleep and did not even know that Alexandria was being occupied by Federal troops. After Ellsworth and his men removed the flag, they descended the staircase, where an awakened and angry Jackson met them.

"I'll take the prize," said Ellsworth as he took the flag and began wrapping it around his body. "Yes, and here is another for you," shouted Jackson as he confronted the soldiers and shot Ellsworth once in the chest with a double barrel shotgun. Before Jackson could fire his other round Francis E. Brownell, one of the soldiers with Ellsworth, shot Jackson in the head and stabbed him with a bayonet.

Ellsworth would be the first real Union soldier killed in the war, and many Northerners, in outrage, made him into a martyr, reciting "Remember Ellsworth" as a "patriotic" slogan. There were some serious issues with this incident, however. For instance, even if the Federals viewed Confederates as rebels, their flag deserved better treatment than it received. Also, it was commonly accepted then (as it is mostly today) that a man's house was his castle. To deny a civilian the right to fly a flag is simply the establishment of tyranny and subjugation. It might have taken five minutes and saved lives if Ellsworth had summoned the owner of the business and properly asked for the removal of the flag. Instead, Ellsworth intruded not for an arrest or a crime being committed, but to *steal* another man's property, something very indicative of how the North conducted itself during the "Civil War." In the end, Jackson was a hero who embodied the fighting spirit of the South. At that time, most

Southerners would have preferred to die on their feet, atop their violated soil, rather than submit to Yankee terror and invasion.

Returning to the original definition of *martyr*—someone killed for his or her beliefs—one could make the case that Ellsworth and Jackson, were more qualified martyrs than John Brown. The fact that John Brown was an abolitionist does not mean that his raid on Harper's Ferry was justified. John Brown broke the law not only by attempting to start a slave insurrection (with no support from slaves) but also by killing an innocent African American man named Hewyard Shepherd. Even before Harper's Ferry, John Brown had committed murders during his "Bleeding Kansas" days. Because of his crimes at Harper's Ferry, Brown was sentenced to death by hanging. Being sentenced to death because of crimes committed does not make someone a martyr.

Ellsworth is a better example of a martyr because <u>in his mind</u> he believed occupying Alexandria and taking down the Confederate flag was his "sacred duty." James Jackson is the best example of a martyr of these three men because his actions show that he was far more committed to his beliefs than either Brown or Ellsworth. Jackson was so devoted to the Confederate cause, and believed so powerfully in it, that he was willing to kill and lose his life just to oppose an invader and keep the Confederate flag flying.

Jackson's engagement with the Union troops was a moment of intense passion and emotion. Southerners attempted to immortalize Jackson by calling him names like "The Alexandria Hero," "The Slayer of Ellsworth," and the "First Martyr for the Cause of Southern

Independence." Southern literature also memorialized Jackson with poems like "Jackson, Our First Martyr":

Yes! He hath won a name,
Deathless for aye to Fame,
Our flag baptized in blood,
Away as with a flood,
Shall sweep the tyrant band,
Whose feet pollute our land.

His martyr-patriot fall
Shall be a trumpet call
For all true men to go
To crush the invading foe
Let not his blood in vain
Cry from the soil they stain
Then Freemen raise the cry,
As Freemen live or die.
Arm, arm you for the fight,
His banner in your sight —
And this your battle-cry,
Jackson and Victory![17]

---

[17] "Jackson, Our First Martyr," by. T.F., Augusta GA, in Alice Fahs, *The Imagined Civil War: Popular Literature of the North and South, 1861-1865* (Chapel Hill: University of North Carolina Press, 2001).

Other poems titled "Jackson, the Alexandria Martyr" and "The Martyr of Alexandria" record Jackson's "impetuous chivalry" and his "fierce, heroic instincts to destroy the insolent invader." Whether Jackson's actions were right or wrong, he stood up for his beliefs and was even willing to die for them. After Jackson exercised his freedom of speech by displaying the Confederate Flag, Federals came in his home, unwarranted, to seize his personal property. While Jackson was asleep, the Federal troops cut down his flag and did not bother to even tell him that they had occupied the city. Did Jackson not have the right to protect his property and honor, or even his beliefs? In the eyes of the United States, certainly not, but the principles Jackson stood up for were very reminiscent of the very ideals for which our American Revolution was fought.

Younger Longest lived in King and Queen County, about 100 miles from Alexandria. News very quickly spread all over as indicated by Fred Fleet, Younger Longest's neighbor, in a letter to his family, calling Jackson a martyr. The various published poems and articles on Jackson, as well as the interest in the Virginia region, suggest that this would have had an impact on Younger Longest. Company I, where Younger served in the 26th Virginia, was known as the "Jackson Grays," in honor of James Jackson. The name was chosen by James Councill, who established the company and was both a leader and teacher for most of the young men in the area.

Put yourself in Younger Longest's shoes for a moment: imagine if you lived in Virginia during the early stages of the Confederacy. A man was killed for defending his right to have the Confederate flag, and the people of the surrounding area all viewed him as a hero and martyr. At the same time, friends, neighbors, family, and teachers would have all been joining the Confederacy. If killing Yankees in defense of Southern ideals constituted martyrdom, then maybe joining the Confederacy was the honorable, right thing to do in Younger's mind.

It seems strange that in 1861, two men were murdered over the removal of the Confederate flag, and now in 2017 there is still a crusade to remove it from public sight. Why is the federal government continually trying to erase history? In James W. Jackson's day, flying the Confederate flag represented nationalism and pride. It was a symbol of separation from the United States. Federal leaders could not stand such. People in the United States saw the flag as a sign of insolence, when it was really more representative of the sentiment of those who flew it in the Confederacy.

If we strip away all the labels and sectional differences, we would see James W. Jackson was simply a man who refused to be subjugated by a much larger, terrorizing force. Even today, the murder of people who wave the Confederate flag continues. More recently, in July 2015, a black man named Anthony Hervey, author of *Why I Wave the Confederate Flag, Written by a Black Man,* was killed in an act of violent road rage. Hervey was an activist who frequently flew the Confederate flag in protest of today's government overreach. While Hervey is just one victim, there have been many people who face violence and criticism *just for their opinions* on the Confederate Flag. The truth is that people of all colors are finally beginning to realize that the government we were left with after the "Civil War" might not be so great after all. Personally, I believe that great majorities of people are beginning to realize that the WBTS was fought with slavery being just a surface issue.

Private John Longest (1827-1864)
Source: *The History of the Longest Family 1652-1992*

John Longest with Matilda Jefferies Longest (1829-1891)
Source: *The History of the Longest Family 1652-1992*

Col. James Calvin Councill
Source: VMI Archives Roster

Colonel Councill's Headstone
King and Queen County, VA
Source: Find A Grave

James W. Jackson
Source: WikiCommons

Elmer Ellsworth
Source: WikiCommons

Marshall House.
Source: Frank Leslie *Famous Leaders and Battle Scenes of the Civil War* (New York, NY: Mrs. Frank Leslie, 1896)

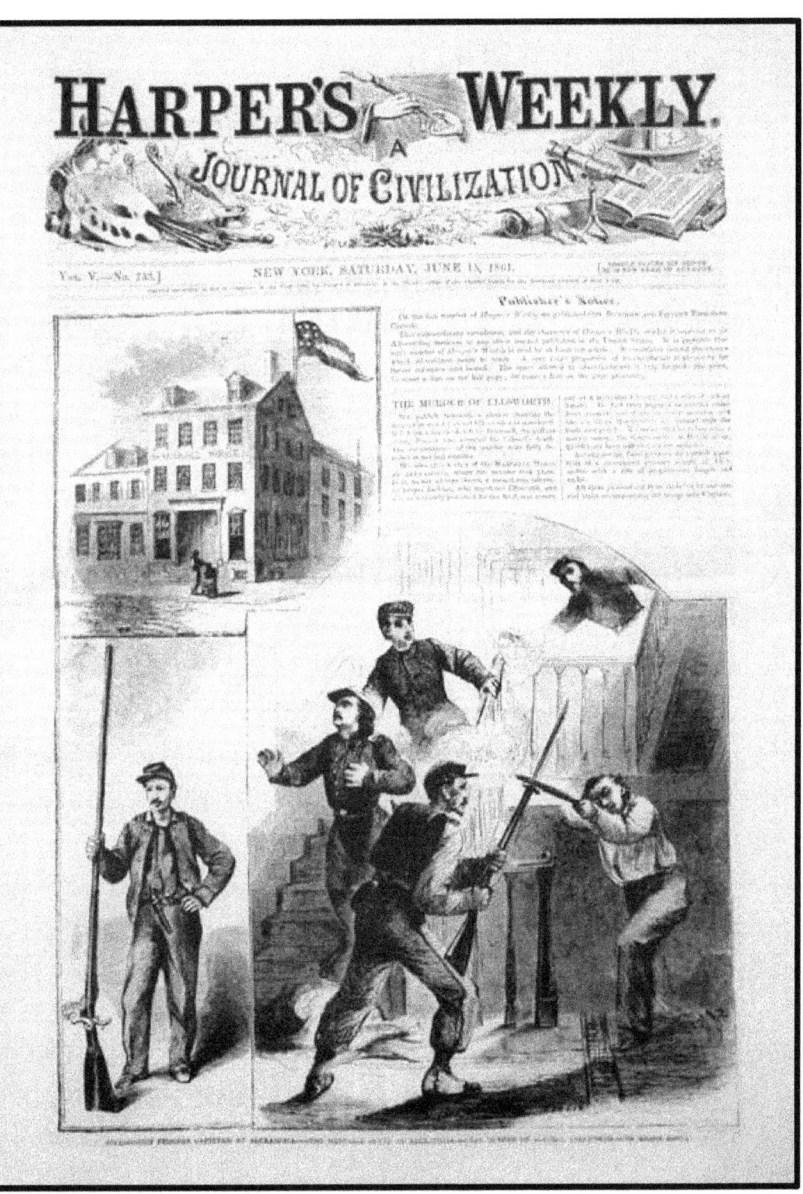

Harper's Weekly "The Marshall House Incident"

Chapter 5
Sight, Sounds, and Civilians at the Siege of Petersburg

PICTURE WHAT CANCER can do to a body. It goes through a person and breaks them down, never resting until every single cell in the body is transformed. If you were to view Petersburg in 1864 as a living organism, you would determine that the effects of Union siege and terror devastated the city at a degree similar to an aggressive cancer.

Petersburg before the War was a center for commerce. With its rail lines and connection by river to the ocean, it was prime real estate for sending Southern exports to the world. Prewar cotton and tobacco were especially booming. The population was estimated at 18,266 at the outbreak of the WBTS, with 3,164 free blacks and 5,680 slaves. The city had beautiful streets, brick sidewalks accompanied by gas lighting, and a municipal water system. Petersburg also had two newspapers, eight banks, a canal system, and roads that connected the city in all directions. As war developed, construction of military hospitals and other war facilities transformed the city.

The day Yankees attacked Petersburg, Sarah Pryor described the sounds and smells: "No lovelier day ever dawned than June 9, 1864. The magnolia glandiflora was in full flower, bee-haunted honey-locusts perfumed the warm air, almost extinguishing the peachy odor of the mycrophylla roses, graceful garlands of Jessamine hung over the trellised front porches."[18] About 9 a.m., Fanny Waddell recalled terrorizing sounds overcoming the beautiful smells as "sound broke upon our ears which palsied our very hearts. It was the sullen roar of cannon and musketry along our lines. And the tolling of the City Hall bell, the signal which summoned grandsires and boys to the defense of their homes."[19]

Shelling of civilians started June 16, 1864. According to Fanny Waddell, "Our inhuman foe without a single warning opened their guns upon us, shelling a city full of defenseless women, children, and old men ... I lay quietly until nearly one o'clock listening to the bursting shells when one exploded so near that the light flashed in my face."[20] Waddell and many other witnesses show that the Union was completely indiscriminate of who or where they were hitting with shells — even women and children were not safe and many were casualties.

This shelling became a normal part of everyday life. A Virginia cavalryman stated that "it was really refreshing to see ladies pass

---

[18] Mrs. Roger A. Pryor, *Reminiscences of Peace and War* (New York: Macmillan, 1905), p. 274.

[19] Diary of Mrs. Charles Waddell. North Carolina Department of Archives and History.

[20] *Ibid.*

coolly along the streets as though nothing unusual was transpiring while the 160-pound shells were howling like hawks of perdition through the smoky air and bursting in the very heart of the city, but they didn't mind it a bit; and even the children would stand and watch, at the sound of the passing shells, to see the explosion, and make funny little speeches about them, as if they had been curious birds flying over their heads."[21]

Petersburg was decimated. Even Yankee newspapers at the time described the destruction vividly. New graves dug all over were a sharp reminder of how dangerous it was to exist as a Southern civilian during Union assault. One man, a physician, described the shelling which almost took his life on August 30: "About ten o'clock I was lying down on a lounge and watching the shells as they flew past the windows ... [Suddenly] two planets of the first magnitude seemed to come together in my face ... I felt myself whirling over in the midst of plaster, lathes, glass, broken timber, and the dust of debris indescribable ... My first sensible thought was, 'I am not killed, it hurts too badly.'"[22]

---

[21] Frank M. Myers, quoted in Noah Andre' Trudeau, *The Last Citadel* (Baton Rouge: LSU Press, 1991), p. 92.

[22] Dr. John F. Claiborne Papers, Library of Virginia Archives.

The terror of being hit by a cannon or mortar shell was never ending. A Confederate engineer declared: "These mortar shells were the most disgusting, low-lived things imaginable … There was not a particle of the sense of honour about them; they would go rolling about and prying into the most private places in a sneaking sort of way."[23] It is interesting that this soldier decided to discuss "particles" of honor. Modern people tend to forget that our ancestors had very keen intuition and senses; this quotation is very telling of the fact that most men knew that fighting for "honor" was a concept that had faded by this point in the war.

Civilians countered with sandbags and cotton bales around the lower floors of buildings. Bombproofs of many designs were built as citizens adjusted to a life of constant terror. More immediate but not so different from the life of constant terror we are exposed to today as Americans. Frances W. Dawson, an English volunteer in the Confederate Army, observed: "Shells frequently fell in or passed over the city, and it was no uncommon thing for old citizens, standing in the street discussing the prospects of the day, to step quietly around a corner until an approaching shell had passed by, and then resume their former place without even suspending their conversation. The basements of houses were used in many instances as bombproofs, the traverses being comprised of mattresses and

---

[23] William W. Blackford, quoted in Trudeau, p. 291.

bedding."[24] The Southern people withstood intense loss and violence at the hands of the North. The grit and unyielding courage they sustained in the face of hardship is something ALL Americans can and should be proud of.

---

[24] Francis Dawson, quoted in Trudeau, p. 96.

Chapter 6

Younger Longest at the Crater

CONFEDERATE AND UNION forces had been fighting for months at Petersburg before the North detonated its eight-thousand- pound mine. This weapon of mass destruction was planted underneath Confederate lines and detonated at approximately 4:44 in the morning of July 30, 1864. The explosion killed nearly a third of the South Carolina regiment that was defending that part of the line and left a blast site that would soon be filled with black and white Union soldiers.

This was an incredible sight, the exact likes of which man probably will never see again. In a day and age when soldiers kill people using drones from the other side of the planet, there is a kind of bloody romanticism about the way this battle was fought. After the mine blew, it left a huge crater that the Union forces charged into amidst the smoke and debris. The walls of the crater were too high to scale and Confederate soldiers surrounded the Union soldiers and shot them down, literally like fish in a barrel. It was not just a violent battle: it was shocking and unprecedented experience. Younger Longest was very close to where the explosion took place and described the scene just a few days later in a letter to his brother James:

> August 4th 1864, Petersburg ... I have no news to write but what you have heard before this time. Saturday was the

awfulest day I ever *saw* … I have wrote to Eliza and stated how it was the best I could. We have buried seven hundred Yankees inside of works, besides what have been got off outside under a flag of truce and they were lying in piles in front of us. It is said to be the greatest fight that have been during the war in such a small place. I *saw* when the dirt commenced flying in the air, it was a *great sight* to see men flying in the air at such a rate and to *see them* lying in the dirt, some covered most up and they was lying in every direction blown to pieces.[25]

Later in his letter, Younger felt compelled to tell his sister that she should be baptized, writing:

I heard that Musco and Manda have been baptized. I wish I could hear something like that about you. I think if you had *seen* as much as I have *seen*, how uncertain life is, you would not put it off any longer.[26]

---

[25] Younger Longest Papers, Library of Virginia Archives.

[26] *Ibid.*

In the months after the Battle of the Crater, Younger went further into the details of the things he had seen during the Siege of Petersburg in another letter. He wrote:

> Petersburg, Oct 25th 1864 ... I think everybody ought to *look* at this war as a solemn and serious thing. *Look* how many lives have been lost. I have *seen* many shot down dead without ever speaking ever again and Oh, ain't it a solemn and a serious thing ... I often think of poor Howard that laid down well and went to sleep and was suddenly killed without ever waking. His shirt and vest was set a fire and burnt most off of him before we could put it out, and his eyes was knocked out. He was black with powder and what an awful *sight* that was and many other things that I have *seen* ... your dear brother until death. Younger Longest[27]

"Poor Howard" refers to Younger's brother, Howard Longest, who was killed by mortar fire in the trenches of Petersburg on July 10, just twenty days before the Battle of the Crater. Howard enrolled for active service on June 13, 1861, and by June 30, 1862, he had been promoted from private to corporal. A muster roll from June 30, 1863,

---

[27] *Ibid.*

shows that he was absent from June 11-June 26 because he had been in pursuit of deserters in his home county of King and Queen.

Imagine the fear that Younger would have felt after seeing his own brother—a man with honor, so devoted to the Confederacy that he had hunted deserters—burned, eyes blown out, probably in pieces. This was something on Younger's mind at the Battle of the Crater, yet the scene of the explosion still overwhelmed him to the point that he viewed it as an awesome *"great sight."* This was an event that made an everlasting impression on his psyche. After The Battle of the Crater, Younger Longest worked as a member of the Pioneer Corps and helped reconstruct the Confederate works. The next event that may have affected his mindset was the death of his cousin, John Longest, who was killed in action in the trenches on December 8, 1864. John was a farmer, who enrolled for the Confederate army on March 4, 1862. Another soldier in the 26th Virginia, Fred Fleet, described his death:

> Dec. 9, 1864 ... We are constantly living now on the line—scarcely a day passes without someone being killed or wounded in the Brigade. On yesterday we lost one of our best men, and a most excellent soldier, John Longest. He was shot through the body by a minie ball, coming in from the picket to the main line, and instantly killed. One here and there is not missed except in some loving circle at

home. Such a *war!* — it deadens the *sensibilities* and *destroys the finer feelings* of us all.[28]

It is incredible, that after experiencing such traumatic events, that Younger Longest continued to fight on. As we will see in the chapters ahead, his religious beliefs and experiences at the Battle of the Crater combined to give him a new outlook on life. Even when the Confederacy's hopes for victory were fading, Younger did not once mention feelings of hopelessness or thoughts of deserting.

TRULY CONSIDER what men like these Confederates experienced; months of siege warfare wore everyone down. Brothers, cousins, and friends were being killed, but Southerners were not willing to give up. The Federals were in a hurry to end things and detonated a four-ton explosive underneath the Southern lines. <u>In their eventual defeat, these Confederates could be the grittiest opponent an attacker has ever faced</u>. In the long history of siege warfare up to that time, had any force of defenders ever withstood such a huge, singular explosion and then successfully repelled an attack as Southerners did at the Battle of the Crater? Furthermore, has any defending force ever withstood such an innovative attack during a siege and continued to fight for so long?

---

[28] *Green Mount*, p. 372.

This says a great deal about the durability, ingenuity, and fire within the Southern people.

In a significant way the Battle of the Crater brought warfare into the modern age. Younger lived in a time just before machine guns, armored tanks, aerial bombardment and explosive missiles. In his day, hot air balloons were the closest things to modern airplanes. This battle showed that there was no more honor in warfare. Killing people and even destroying the ground beneath them was the new logic of how to fight wars. This mindset of blowing up things to kill your enemy has carried over into destroying buildings full of people and is probably the mindset held by mass-shooters and bombers who kill innocent people today.

Although the explosion itself did not kill Union troops, they became victims of their own attack by running directly into the Crater. Perhaps the most controversial decision in the battle was for the Union command to head the attack with black soldiers. Not only were black soldiers paid less than white soldiers in the Union army, but they were also segregated and used as cannon fodder on many occasions. The main reason they were chosen to spearhead the assault after the explosion of the mine was that Union generals had no idea what to expect.

The black regiment was originally chosen to attack first, but Union leadership decided against it because they did not want negative press during the 1864 election. They ended up drawing straws and the worst regiment drew the shortest. The black soldiers ended up suffering the most casualties because they were sent in after the battle had turned for the Union. One source based out of

Long Island, NY stated the following about Union conduct at the battle: "Many of the white Union soldiers believed that if they were captured near black troops they would be executed." Captain Kilmer of a New York regiment said that Union soldiers "bayoneted blacks who fell into the crater. This was in order to preserve whites from Confederate vengeance."[29]

The same basic situation can be seen at the Union assault on Ft. Wagner in South Carolina. Popularized in the movie *Glory*, it depicts the 54th Massachusetts black soldiers as the heroes who lead the attack on Ft. Wagner (a well-deserved depiction) — while ignoring the fact that they were completely expendable to the Union army. People can say what they will about Southerners, but they never sent massive numbers of "free" blacks to their death like the Union army. According to the logic of today, undermining as it was done at Petersburg would absolutely be considered a terrorist tactic.

If "terrorists" are defined as people who fly planes into buildings and blow up cars full of people, what did that make Yankees that detonated a four-ton bomb underneath sleeping Southerners, then used their "expendable" soldiers to spearhead a surprise attack? In

---

[29] Young, Patrick, Esq. "A Volcano in Virginia: The Battle of the Crater," *Long Island WINS*, September 10, 2014. https://longislandwins.com/columns/immigrants-civil-war/ a-volcano-in-virginia-the- battle-of-the-crater/

a way, Younger Longest and every other Confederate at the Crater was the victim of a terrorist attack, the size of which would captivate today's media for ages.

To be fair, however, the use of land mines was not something unknown to Confederates. Gabriel Rains, a Confederate brigadier general, is often credited with inventing the first modern land mines. These explosives were crude by today's standards and were mainly implemented on the coast to protect Confederate port cities like Charleston, Savannah, Mobile, etc. Thousands were buried, being easily constructed of simple iron containers with gunpowder, a fuse, and a detonation cap. Being hard to spot, mines were a problem for Union soldiers; reportedly, William Tecumseh Sherman forced Confederate POWs to march in front of Union soldiers as victims for any possible mines. He and other generals like George B. McClellan were quick to denounce Confederate mines as barbarism and murder. Did these Union men contradict themselves by using a massive land mine to blow up sleeping Confederates at Petersburg?

Federal use of mines was in stark contrast to the way Confederates used them. The Southern people were a culture of honor and did not use weapons like mines in an offensive manner. The South used them extensively as a defensive tool because they were outnumbered, surrounded on almost all fronts, and blockaded. Would using mines to defend your homeland really be so "barbarous" in a situation like that? It seems ironic that the Confederates successfully defeated the first act of Yankee Terrorism at the Battle of the Crater, but lost the WBTS. *Southerners were literally, in an instant, the victims of a weapon of mass destruction* and went on to immediately defeat their attackers. However, their inability to cope with a world where these tactics were accepted would be their downfall.

Today, Americans are forced to live in a world where we must be exposed to terror every day. Younger Longest was walking around Virginia in 1864 expecting "to be blown up at any time" by the Federal government of the United States. There are people walking all over the world, right at this second, who could say the very same thing! The fact that we can even draw such a parallel shows the importance of telling Younger's story.

Chapter 7

The Sight and Smell of Terror

IMMEDIATELY AFTER THE BATTLE of the Crater, the air in Petersburg was saturated with light dust. The earth beneath the soldiers was so barren and destroyed that it brightly reflected the sunlight. Soldiers on both sides found their clothes, supplies, food and drinks covered in sticky dust. Both sides were feeling worn down and exhausted, but the Union had twice the manpower and almost surrounded Petersburg. Even with victory at the Battle of the Crater, Southerners were still fearful of another Union undermining. As discussed in the Introduction, our thoughts are everything. When someone says they fear something, what he or she is more literally saying is, "I am thinking fearful thoughts, and those thoughts are sending vibrations through my body that make me *feel* scared."

After reading in the last chapter about what soldiers saw at the Crater, we now have a good foundation to build upon what might have been in their minds during their experiences at Petersburg. In this chapter, we will examine Younger Longest's written thoughts and discuss the physical feelings he might have experienced. In a letter of August 4, 1864, just days after The Battle of the Crater, he wrote:

Dear Brother ... I am well at this time as I could expect to be for the place I am in. The weather is very hot and dry and we have no shade to go under. Nor can we get any fresh air. Nor any water that is fit to drink. I have received your letter and money safely, I am very much obliged to you for it but I don't know when I shall get any to pay it back. I am very sorry to hear you are got to go in service, but I hope you all will not have to stay long before this cruel war will end and all of us that are spared will return home to our family and friends.[30]

There are some very telling lines here that show both what Younger was going through and the type of man that he was. First, we can tell that he was physically *feeling* completely exhausted from the trench warfare at Petersburg. He openly laments the heat and dryness, adding that there is no shade, fresh air, or water. Despite these conditions and the added trauma of the Battle of the Crater, Younger felt compelled to thank his brother for sending him money. In a display of honor, Younger also comments that he did not know if or when he would be able to pay his brother back. This shows that he was "feeling" two different types of emotion: *gratitude* and *fear*. The fact that he thanks his brother in such a serious time shows he was indeed grateful. That he did not know when he would be able

---

[30] Younger Longest Papers, Library of Virginia Archives.

to pay it back reflects his personal honor and the *fear* he was experiencing. Later in the same letter, Younger mentioned :

> Grant is undermining in two or three more places along our line. We may expect to be blown up at any time.

Younger also detailed how cruel the war was and referred to his hope that he, his family, and his friends would be spared. These are telltale signs that he may have expected to die; Confederates at Petersburg faced constant artillery shelling, and after the Battle of the Crater, getting blown up from a mine was a very real threat. This meant that Younger probably never *felt* safe; at any time he could be blown up from above or below. Another pervasive sensation for Confederates at Petersburg would have been the *smell*. In a letter written home over a month after the crater, Fred Fleet wrote about the smell of corpses in the Crater:

> September 9, 1864 ... On Monday we came back to the trenches and took our position within a hundred & fifty yards of the famous mine, a part of the brigade reaching it, and cooking and sleeping just over the pits in which so many dead—black and white Yankees are buried. A large quantity of lime has been sprinkled over the bodies & 20 feet of dirt thrown upon that & then another layer of lime, which effectually smothers any unpleasant odor, which

might naturally be supposed to issue from such a large number of corpses.[31]

At the same time, Younger Longest was battling intense odors of his own. In his same letter from August 4, 1864, Younger described traveling back to Virginia from the siege of Charleston and wrote:

> I am most always thinking about you all and know it is hard times with you all, to what you have been used to, but this is a time that you can all live well [compared] to what we soldiers are doing. Lyin' in trenches day and night and never be relieved to wash our shirts. We have to wear them three and four weeks and more before we can get the chance to pull them off to wash ... I have not slept with my shoes nor clothes off since I reached Virginia from Charleston ... Catharine, I shall claim you for one or two pieces of your old hard soap if you have the chance to send it to me. I don't get soap to wash my hands.

The smells these Confederate soldiers faced would have been repugnant. Imagine sitting on top of hundreds of dead bodies, and simultaneously wearing clothes that had not been taken off or washed for weeks at a time. Without soap these men faced strong odors that were nauseating at times. It is very interesting that of all

---

[31] *Green Mount*, p. 291.

the things Younger Longest could have asked for in his letters home, soap was the most important thing on his mind. Many men wrote home asking for food, clothing, and blankets. The fact that Younger was asking his sister for soap may well indicate that a *"feeling"* of uncleanness was widespread throughout the Confederate trenches. These men sat in the mud for nearly ten months and would be shot to death by Yankee sharpshooters or blown apart by artillery if they left the trenches.[32]

Just as the smell of death and body odor was common for Confederates, so were the sounds of invasion. In the trenches, Fred Fleet detailed the back and forth shelling at Petersburg as "such a furious cannonade I have never heard before." Soldiers on both sides were scared and exhausted. At times, the anxiety could only be relieved through the sound of music. In a letter to his mother, Fred Fleet describes how Confederates and Yankees played music during the downtimes:

> We have plenty of Yankee music and by going a few hundred yards to the rear of the trenches, several bands can

---

[32] Doubtless many or most men on both sides drew comfort from the smell and taste of tobacco in pipes, cigars, chewing plugs, and snuff. Tobacco had been for over two centuries Virginia's most important product and Petersburg was a tobacco marketing and manufacturing center.

be heard from the different parts of the line. Among the tunes we hear frequently are "Hail, Columbia," the "Star-Spangled Banner," "When this Cruel War is Over." Their bands are superior to ours as the majority of them were formed before the war, and their instruments are much better than any we can procure.[33]

Younger Longest experienced great hardship during the siege of Petersburg. Horrific feelings, smells and sounds saturated the Confederate trenches. Feelings of anxiety and fear spread fast as soldiers faced destruction from above and below. The sounds of approaching enemy were entrenched in his mind—"The Yankees are Coming!" became a sound of <u>terror</u>. But the fear did not disable the will to fight the invader. The sight, smell, and sound of the approaching enemy were entrenched in Confederate minds.

---

[33] *Green Mount*, p. 361.

Chapter 8

Virginia Tasting Defeat

IN MODERN TIMES, THE SOUTH is known as a land of comfort food. Most people associate Southern cooking with fried chicken, collards, biscuits and the like. This is a phenomenon that has been popularized in the wake of television cooks like Paula Deen and restaurants like KFC and Cracker Barrel. Before the WBTS in Virginia, abundant food functioned as a type of currency for everyday people. Studying what Virginians tasted before the WBTS, it becomes evident that what people ate depended on their day-to-day activities. What a young man ate after a day of working at a neighbor's farm was different from what he would eat with his family on a special occasion. Sometimes people were paid for hard labor in food; other times, some food materials were even used as medicine. The taste of Virginians was natural and simple, but by the time of the events at Petersburg, it would be completely ravaged by total war, siege tactics, and Union terror.

When times were good before the war, many Virginians enjoyed a pallet of healthy and wholesome snacks. Apples were a staple food in Younger Longest's community. In local sources, including Younger's own letters, you find apples frequently mentioned. Bennie Fleet, in a letter to his brother Fred in June of 1860, described how a snack before the war would have included "Nice mellow apples, biscuit, butter, milk and honey. With cider made of ripe apples to drink."³⁴ The Fleets also ate lemons, plums, muskmelons, watermelons, dried peaches, and candied ginger quite regularly. These simple fruits were exchanged for farm-hand tasks like building fences or digging ditches. Other easy snacks would have been eaten throughout the day while working outside and included shortcakes, cornbread, honey in the comb, buttermilk, whortleberries, and bread loaves with various jams. For a more high protein intake, many Virginians looked to bullfrog legs, chinquapins, possums and squirrels (squirrels were best in soup).

Meals that were eaten for dinner and supper usually involved more protein, more food choices, and even dessert. The Fleet family enjoyed one great meal they had in February of 1861 that included "Ham and turnip greens at the head, turkey at the foot, very fine shoat, hominy, rice, sweet potatoes, baked and fried shad, and oyster soup."³⁵ For dessert, they chose among ice cream, jelly, cakes, and gooseberry pies. Another delicious dinner in April of 1861 was described as having included "duck, bacon and cabbage, corn, cucumbers, onions, Irish potatoes, and bread in abundance."³⁶ Sources make it clear that Virginians before the war had a diet that

---

[34] *Ibid.*, p. 32.

[35] *Ibid.*, p. 69.

[36] *Ibid.*, p. 81.

was healthy, well balanced, and provided almost completely by nature and their own effort. Often, the scope of the meals depended on what kind of work was done that day and what had been bartered with relatives and neighbors.

Natural foods and plants were important to Virginians as a type of currency, but they also were used frequently for medicinal purposes. If a hornet stung someone, wetting and applying tobacco to the sting was a quick remedy. For foot pain, a natural reliever was found by bathing the feet with a pine top, mullein (a plant) and fish brine boiled together. Respiratory congestion could be fixed by an onion poultice. Steaming onions, put on a white cloth for poultice, were breathed in to clear the sinuses—afterward the onions could be eaten with salt, pepper, and butter for a delicious snack. Virginians also had a natural remedy for dysentery, a major killer during the WBTS. According to Dr. Benjamin Fleet, in a letter to his son Fred at the outbreak of war in September of 1861, it could be cured by taking "Blue mass and opium pills, followed by epsom salts and Jamaica ginger the next day." After ingesting the concoction, Dr. Fleet advised: "Avoid cold water, instead boil gum with sassafras pith and drink hot." Dr. Fleet also suggested that drinking hot sage and ginger tea, or sage with extract ginger, then bathing the feet in hot water with mustard and salt could prevent measles.[37]

As the WBTS raged on, Southern soldiers and civilians alike were able to taste the difference. As the Union army strangled Petersburg, soldiers like Younger Longest craved apples and the simple, healthy food they once ate at home. Most of the time soldiers were reduced to a diet of fried bacon and bread, with an almost complete absence of vegetables. Sometimes fortunate Confederates would receive goods from families. For example, on different occasions, the Fleet family sent their son 12 dozen herrings, a quarter lamb, lamb's head pie, loaf bread, biscuit, corn bread, butter, milk, strawberries and apples, as well as clothes.

These types of gifts were rare and when a soldier did receive them they were shared with comrades. A true delicacy for Confederates during the siege would have been a basic stew with onions and beef. The situation in Petersburg was so dire that fresh beef could only be obtained after Confederate General Wade Hampton rode behind enemy lines and rustled 2,000 Union cattle in an episode dubbed "The Beefsteak Raid."

Most of the Southern civilians in Petersburg were facing just as much hardship as the soldiers. They knew how terrorizing a Union

---

[37] *Ibid.*, p. 90.

siege could be for noncombatants. During Ulysses S. Grant's siege at Vicksburg, Southern civilians were reduced to eating rats and mules and living in bombproof caves and some were killed and wounded. Sarah Pryor, in Petersburg with her children, remembered: "with all our starvation we never ate rats, mice or mule meat, we managed to exist on peas, bread, and sorghum. We could buy a little milk, and we mixed it with a drink made from roasted and ground corn. The latter, in the grain, was scarce."[38]

"Starvation parties" became a popular event for civilians during their downtime. These events were put on by the civilians as a way of keeping morale high during siege. Dr. John Herbert Claiborne wrote: "There were parties, starvation parties, as they were called, on account of the absence of refreshments impossible to be obtained; ball followed ball, and the soldiers met and danced with his lady at night, and on the morrow danced the dance of death in the deathly trenches out on the line."[39] Customary imported goods like coffee were impossible to get. So hard was it to find the warm drink that Confederate soldiers traded plugs of chewing tobacco with Union

---

[38] Mrs. Roger A Pryor, *Reminiscences*, p. 327.

[39] Dr. John H. Claiborne Papers, Library of Virginia Archives.

soldiers to get a little coffee, while civilians in Petersburg made their own brew of chicory, dried peas, and beets.[40]

Despite the hunger and starvation Confederates faced, they ill continued to fight hard. While some deserted, the overwhelming desire in the ranks was never to see the South subdued. This resolve was reflected in the statements of Virginia's popular former governor Henry A. Wise. Five years before the war, Wise had called for Virginia to secede from the Union. Even though he had no [41]military training, he was made a General because of his reputation. Virginians loved Wise and believed him when he said they would have to go through, as Dr. Ben Fleet described in a letter on December 3, 1863, to his son Fred, "a baptism of fire and blood" before their independence could be achieved.

In a speech Wise gave on June 12, 1864, he said:

> Petersburg is to be and shall be defended on her outer walls, on her inner lines, at her corporation bounds, on every street, and around every temple of God and altar of man, in her every heart, until the blood of that heart is spilt.

---

[40] Robert B. Pamplin, *Prelude to Surrender: The Pamplin Family and the Siege of Petersburg* (Petersburg: Master Media, 1995), p. 223.

[41] *Green Mount*, p. 223.

Roused by this spirit to this pitch of resolution, we will fight the enemy at every step, and Petersburg is safe.[42]

These extreme words show that people in the Virginia truly believed they were being terrorized by the Union and had to fight, regardless of how hungry they were.

---

[42] *Petersburg Express*, June 13, 1864.

Chapter 9
Southerners in a Cold World

AS OF THE YEAR 2017, it has become fair game to take down or slander anything Confederate. The removal of monuments in states throughout the South has seemingly become a preoccupation for many. Before I became educated on the topic, I had no knowledge regarding this controversy other than the Confederate flag flying in front of the South Carolina state house in Columbia. In college, I had a liberal professor at the University of South Carolina walk my class to the state house for our last meeting. We discussed, at length, the many perceptions of the flag. He referred to it many times as the "rebel" flag and made sure we all understood that the "Civil War" was about slavery. We were made to believe the flag did not belong, and this was about four years before the AME church shooting in Charleston that caused mass hysteria over Confederate flags across the country.

Growing up in South Carolina, I've always been around this history and its many interpretations. Even when I initially discovered intentions to remove or discredit these Confederate relics, I had no real reason to have any second thoughts. However, discovering my heritage and witnessing its current destruction changed things for me. Researching my ancestors and learning how they suffered at the hands of the Union, I realized that maybe these monuments were more important than my liberal professors had taught. That is why I decided to write this book, in an attempt to give humanity to these "rebels" that many people only associate with "white supremacy." If the academics that oppose Confederate symbols stopped and took a look, they would find little real evidence of "white supremacy" among the men who fought for the South. My own ancestors had nothing to leave behind except their accounts of having been terrorized by Yankees. If these modern pontiffs, politicians, and activists really did their homework, they would find that Confederates were a people that just wanted to be independent. They were not interested in subjugating or invading anyone, they simply wanted to be left alone. This final chapter looks to show that even in their eventual demise, Confederates were honorable, faithful, and far more interested in peace than our modern narrative describes.

By the time of the Siege of Petersburg, many in the Confederate armies fought without basic necessities like shoes; some regiments. At points when ammunition was low, some Southerners resorted to throwing bats and rocks to defend their lines. The fact that these Southerners were willing to face a larger, better-equipped force deserves more appreciation and study. Their resolve and grit are truly remarkable even today.

Confederates would only be defeated after a complete change in how war was fought: wreaking "total war" on a population of civilians. In Younger Longest's last known letter, he begins by detailing how dire circumstances had become in the months of siege after the Battle of the Crater:

Petersburg, Oct 25th 1864. Dear Brother, I seat myself this beautiful Sabbath morning to write you a few lines to let you hear I am yet alive and well except cold. Most always, from sleeping in the dew on the naked ground, all the frost and dew falls on me. We have orders to sleep with our cartridge box on and our gun at our head. Lieutenant Latane is at the hospital quite sickly with yellow jaundice. Griffin have been quite sick at the hospital but I seen him yesterday and he was getting better of his chills and fevers.[43]

Conditions were quickly deteriorating for the Confederate forces. Younger and his regiment had to be ready to fight at a second's notice, literally sleeping with their boots on and gun by their heads. In the dead of winter, they faced harsh weather, similar to what Washington and his men faced at Valley Forge. Younger, in the same letter of October 25, 1864, described desperation just to *feel* warm in the trenches:

The Weather has been quite cold here for several days and we can't get but little wood, none but what they give us and that is very little. I don't know what we will do this

---

[43] Younger Longest Papers, Library of Virginia Archives.

winter for wood and clothing. Our company has not drawn but two blankets this fall and *all* is without.

Soldiers in Younger's regiment depended entirely on their grit to survive. These Confederates were ready to fight at any second and braved freezing winters with few supplies. Are there not some evident parallels between what these men went through and what our American founding fathers went through? Younger described both the difficulty to obtain food and its scarcity in his October 25th letter:

We get one pound of flour, enough bread for a day and night, and that makes us sore and sometimes seven little biscuits and if we buy, we have to give two dollars for a pound of flour or two dollars for a pone[44] of light bread and that is small. Sweet potatoes is twelve dollars a peck, cabbage five dollars per head, dry peas two dollars per quart, bacon ten dollars a pound, butter ten dollars, eggs ten dollars, and so on ….

The price to survive in the Confederacy became increasingly expensive as Northern terror devastated their land. While William

---

[44] Pone is an unleavened cornbread in the form of flat cakes or loaves. It was made by North American Indians with water and cooked in hot ashes.

Tecumseh Sherman was rampaging through the South on his "March to the Sea," Philip Sheridan had orders from Ulysses Grant to destroy all provisions and means of forage in the Shenandoah Valley. Fred Fleet described this in a letter to his mother, on February 5, 1865 and said, "the wretch is literally obeying the instructions of his superior and is burning all the barns, mills, etc."[45] The letter also described Grant as an "unmitigated scoundrel," something very indicative of how Southern people felt about these Northern terror tactics.

When the Federals made a breakthrough in one part of the lines in March, this "total war" descended on Petersburg with a vengeance. Henry T. Bahnson, a North Carolina sharpshooter, described seeing women and children blown in pieces in the street.[46] A Confederate captain, John C. Gorman, just a few miles west of the scene witnessed: "The whole heavens in our rear were lit up in lurid glare that added intensity to the blackness before us...It was as if the gases chained in the earth had at least found vent and the

---

[45] *Green Mount*, p. 345.

[46] Henry T. Bahnson, *The Last Days of the War* (The North Carolina Booklet: Vol. 2, Issue 12: April 1903) p.1-23.

general conflagration of the world was at hand." This was not war, but hell on earth.[47]

With much of the South in ruins, facing destruction from above and below, Younger Longest still clung to the thoughts of his family and his faith, as indicated below:

> I *think* a good deal about you all and *see* a great deal of uneasiness about my family. I have no money to send them nor none for myself. I don't know what they will do for shoes this winter, I can't help them none and it troubles me more than everything else but I have no right to grumble, I don't reckon.

The grit within Younger is very apparent in the statement above. Even though he faced death, literally at any moment, he understood that he had no right to complain. He was content knowing that he and his family were alive. He also kept pushing on and fighting, never giving up in his country's ideals. His country's downfall was out of his hands. Experiencing the end of the Confederacy was a very harsh reality for Younger and the South as a whole. Religious leaders had said that Confederate defeat would mean "the progress of civilization will be thrown back a century," and that "Southerners

---

[47] J. C. Gorman, *Lee's Last Campaign, With an Accurate History of Stonewall Jackson's Last Wound*. (Raleigh, NC: W.B. Smith & Co.: 1866).

must trust God to save them" because "the Yankee invaders have shown how utterly bestial they can be."[48] Younger had experienced the hate and terror of the Yankees first hand, and when he realized his survival was out of his hands, he turned to religion to free his mind, as indicated near the end of his October 25, 1864, letter:

> I want to come home worse than I ever did in my life to see you all but it seems like a bad chance to look at things at this time. <u>But I trust in the Lord that he will spare me still longer and enable me to come to see my Family and all of you</u>...The Lord have spared them and myself during this long and cruel war and <u>I have no right to grumble</u> and I pray it may soon come to an end so all that are spared may return home. But if it be not God's will we must be resigned to whatever He thinks best and let us all try and prepare ourselves to meet Him in peace and where there will be no war and parting will be no more.

This thought of defeat by Yankee terror was a legitimate fear in the mind of the South. Robert L. Dabney, one of the South's leading theologians, wrote at the time of defeat that Virginia would be "completely Yankeeized," and that "the honor, the hospitality, the integrity, everything which constituted Southern character is gone forever."[48] In another speech Dabney said that Confederate defeat

---

[48] Speech by Reverend J. Henry Smith of North Carolina in December 1861.

was proof that God uses infidels to chastise His people and that the righteous side is not always victorious in war.

Whether or not Younger Longest agreed with Dabney is unclear. However, there was undoubtedly an ominous and pervasive feeling that society would be filled with *terror* if the Yankees won the WBTS. He experienced so many traumas at the hands of the United States that it is now incredible to read about his grit and his determination to see the thing through. It is admirable that he fought with such conviction, against this terror, with all the odds stacked against him. In the end, only his faith would set his mind at ease. In his October 25, 1864 letter, Younger wrote:

> I thank God that these things have brought me to see my sins and pray for them and get pardon for them, as I trust in the Lord he have forgave me and caused me to believe in Him & love Him and all of people….

In closing the letter, Younger added a prayer that he had taken from a hymnal. It was called "So Let our Lips and Lives Express," written by Isaac Watts in 1707. Notice the sensory descriptions in the hymn used by Younger:

So let our lips and lives express
The holy gospel we profess
So let our works and virtues shine
To prove thy doctrine divine

Thus shall we best proclaim abroad
The honors of our savior God

When the Salvation reigns within
And grace subdues the power of sin

The violence and terror that Younger had to live with could only be borne once he reached a higher plane of understanding. At the beginning of the war, martyrs that killed people in defense of Southern heritage inspired him. He witnessed growing violence and the secession of his state and joined most other men his age by enlisting in the infantry to ward off Northern invaders. By the war's end, Younger understood how fragile life could be. The only way his mind could actually express these *feelings* was through prayer and spirituality. For these reasons, I think his story is a very powerful one.

Honoring a Confederate ancestor today has become taboo. If Younger and many others fought so bravely, why is it so difficult now, in 2017, to honor Confederate ancestors? Drawing a comparison between Younger's Virginia and George Washington's Virginia arouses more questions. It could be argued that the United States, during the WBTS, treated the South worse than the British treated Americans during our Revolution.

Regardless of whether or not one thinks the Union resorted to terrorism by our modern standards, the fact remains: the United States, in an attempt to "preserve the Union," bombed, starved, and flat-out murdered other Americans. The Union destroyed the means of living of thousands of civilians, black and white, and suppressed free speech, using its size and power to enforce unpopular actions. Younger fought in a time where it was patriotic to stand up for your state, family, and local way of life. Although it may be discouraged today, his thoughts and actions deserve further study. As Americans, any one of us should be able to celebrate his story.

Going inside the mind of Younger Longest gives a deep and detailed look at the grit, faith, and resolve that make the Southern people so unique.

About the Author

MICHAEL MARTIN is a teacher, writer, and historian with experience working in both public and private schools. He currently resides in Charleston, South Carolina, with his wife and daughter, where he specializes in early Virginia history, genealogy, and the emerging field of sensory history.

From Shotwell Publishing

IF YOU ENJOYED THIS BOOK, perhaps some of our other titles will pique your interest. The following titles are currently available from Shotwell at Amazon and all major online book retailers.

JOYCE BENNETT

Maryland, My Maryland: The Cultural Cleansing of a Small Southern State

JERRY BREWER

Dismantling the Republic

ANDREW P. CALHOUN, JR.

My Own Darling Wife: Letters From a Confederate Volunteer [John Francis Calhoun]

JOHN CHODES

Segregation: Federal Policy or Racism?

Washington's KKK: The Union League During Southern Reconstruction

PAUL C. GRAHAM

Confederaphobia: An American Epidemic

When the Yankees Come: Former South Carolina Slaves Remember Sherman's Invasion

JOSEPH JAY

Sacred Conviction: The South's Stand for Biblical Authority

JAMES R. KENNEDY

Dixie Rising: Rules for Rebels

JAMES R. & WALTER D. KENNEDY

Punished with Poverty: The Suffering South

PHILIP LEIGH

The Devil's Town: Hot Spring During the Gangster Era

MICHAEL MARTIN

Southern Grit: Sensing the Siege at Petersburg

CHARLES T. PACE

Lincoln As He Was

Southern Independence. Why War?

JAMES RUTLEDGE ROESCH

From Founding Fathers to Fire Eaters: The Constitutional Doctrine of States' Rights in the Old South

KIRKPATRICK SALE

Emancipation Hell: The Tragedy Wrought By Lincoln's Emancipation Proclamation

KAREN STOKES

A Legion of Devils: Sherman in South Carolina

Carolina Love Letters

JOHN VINSON

Southerner, Take Your Stand!

CLYDE N. WILSON

Lies My Teacher Told Me: The True History of the War for Southern Independence

SOUTHERN READER'S GUIDE

The Old South: 50 Essential Books (I)

THE WILSON FILES

The Yankee Problem: An American Dilemma (1)

Nullification: Reclaiming Consent of the Governed (2)

Annals of the Stupid Party: Republicans Before Trump (3)

Green Altar Books (Literary Imprint)

RANDALL IVEY

A New England Romance & Other SOUTHERN Stories

JAMES EVERETT KIBLER

Tiller (Clay Bank County, IV)

KAREN STOKES

Belles: A Carolina Romance

Honor in the Dust

The Immortals

The Soldier's Ghost: A Tale of Charleston

GOLD-BUG (Mystery & Suspense Imprint)

MICHAEL ANDREW GRISSOM

Billie Jo

BRANDI PERRY

Splintered: A New Orleans Tale

MARTIN L. WILSON

To Jekyll and Hide

Free Book Offer

Sign-up for new release notification and receive a FREE DOWNLOADABLE EDITION of *Lies My Teacher Told Me: The True History of the War for Southern Independence* by Dr. Clyde N. Wilson by visiting FreeLiesBook.com or by texting the word "Dixie" to 345345. You can always unsubscribe and keep the book, so you've got nothing to lose!

SOUTHERN WITHOUT APOLOGY

www.ingramcontent.com/pod-product-compliance
Lightning Source LLC
Chambersburg PA
CBHW070654050426
42451CB00008B/349